YEAR OF THE CREATOR

A Guide to Create Your
Vision with God.

Denisha Ferguson

By Denisha Ferguson

Copyright © 2021

All rights reserved. No part of this book may be reproduced or used in any manner without the prior written permission of the copyright owner, Denisha Ferguson

except for the use of brief quotations in a book review.

To request permissions, contact the publisher at info@yearofthecreator.com

First paperback edition by UnZIP and Create International LLC

Layout and Edited by Christian Shepreneur Academy

Cover and Back Design by Michael Weston

Photograph of Author by MMW

Introduction

The year of the creator is acknowledging God as the ultimate creator, who created us in His image. It's knowing God gave us the power to create, and that divine power comes forth when we are creating with God.

When I started saying "it's the Year of the Creator" before writing this book, others who heard it took it as meaning the year to create from more of a personal stance. Like it's my year to finally do "it" and "it" is defined as whatever goal they had. The visions and goals you have are for a reason. Some of the ideas may be seeds planted by others. Like your mom was a doctor and wants you to be a doctor. Some of your ideas are going to be from your experiences, so you have to watch why you are pursuing it and if it's something you're doing to prove yourself or because you see others doing it. And then there are the ideas that are God given. So, we want to get to the heart of those visions and pursue those. So, yes! Going after your dreams, goals, visions (however you define them) is what's discussed in this book! God wants you to create, but not from someone else's vision, not on your own, but with God.

The year of the creator saying can also be seen as being amongst other year declarations. Like the year of clarity, the year of abundance, or the year of a specific color - but it's more than that.

I pray you see that God is always present and working in your life, whether it seems that way or not. What God needs from us is to show up to help do His work (not make it happen). God is the driver and He wants us to help make the change. To help create solutions. To help create that idea. To help build a platform. To help with a need. He wants you to become what He designed you to be and in showing up, God's power in you is released. So release what is in you to create change, love, and develop solutions. This year can still be the year of clarity, abundance, and pivots. The year you finish school, start a business, or expand your family. The foundation of each and every year is this: it's the year of the Creator. Every year is the year of God who is creating all around you, in others, and working through and in you. But the KEY is to create *with* GOD.

No matter what you are facing, God is there. By taking steps with God each day, He is preparing you for your purpose. Will you take this journey with Him? The beauty is that no matter who you are or what you've been through - God is already with you and you can start creating with Him at any moment. You can start right now. Which is actually what you are doing by consuming key tools, like this book. In knowing this, no other decision you make should be made without God. And how do you make decisions with God? You seek God, set your mind and heart on God and ask for guidance.

From the Author

The Year of the Creator was God given. I am grateful for the experience. While writing it. I went through a process of shedding limitations that I didn't realize I placed on myself. It also challenged what I was writing. I know it was my authenticity check. I've heard this so many times. What you put out is often what you need the most. Yes, this book is what I needed and it will continue to be a classic with me each year as a reminder that it is the …. The Year of the Creator. The year that God blessed me with. My intention is that it blesses you to know that God is with you and will never leave you. Today you can take steps to create those ideas you have with God and God will work it out in your favor at the appointed time God says.

Contents

Chapter 1: The Year of the Creator 1

Chapter 2: Designed a Success 5

Chapter 3: Purpose Acceleration 10

Chapter 4: Say Yes 12

Chapter 5: Perspective Shift... 15

Chapter 6: Plan... 19

Chapter 7: The Power of Praying and Fasting 24

Chapter 8: Where to Start.. 30

Chapter 9: Faith in the Midst 34

Chapter 10: Creating Resources and Opportunities 39

Chapter 11: God's Plan for You is Bigger 45

Chapter 12: Take Steps Today.. 50

11 Keys to Release the Creator in You 53

About the Author 64

CHAPTER 1

The Year of the Creator

Get Excited! God has been ready to create with you. God needs you to believe and have faith to carry out His vision knowing that He is right there with you, and you already have the victory. You are already a success. You are enough.

> *"But without faith, it is impossible to please Him, for he who comes to God must believe that He is and that He is a rewarder of those who diligently seek Him."* Hebrews 11:6 (KJV)

If you are coming from a place of uncertainty and tensions are high, let's get back to the basics and re-center our thoughts making sure they are on God. There will be challenging times, but there is a difference between doing it on your own, and having peace and direction when doing it with God. This is the Year of the Creator. Every day leads up to the year and each New Year is still the year of the creator. God is omnipotent and omnipresent. God doesn't live in our time or come in our timing. Yet we do experience time. We experience hours, days, months, and years. So by remembering that it all leads up to God's vision for us, we can help redefine time and not put those pressures on ourselves. We can move in a flow that knows God will be right on time. Just because you are a certain age, doesn't mean it's over for you. Just because you have not reached a certain goal, doesn't mean it's not coming. God has big plans for you and it isn't over. It's just beginning. Stay Excited!

So, how do we focus on God's plan for us when there are so many things going on in the world and so many things we have to do?

Seek to channel that focus on how you can show love and be a light in the world. You are still aware of the reality. You see the bill, you see the circumstance but more than that you see the vision of God. You are determined to pursue it despite the circumstance because you know God made you for greatness and no one can take that away from you. Only you can. You are the only person who can sabotage you or give power to outside things that keep you from doing the will of God.

Remember what you don't do is just as important as what you do. So don't overlook that. I could be working on something else right now or doing something as simple as being at the grocery store wandering and shopping, diverting to other tasks, and filling my agenda with things that don't matter. What matters right now is me releasing what is in my mind to put in this book. When finished, it will be a tool for you to use as you hear from God. Yes, I need to go to the grocery store at times, but oftentimes that can take 4 hours! The question is: what are you filling God's time up with that is not conducive to carrying out what God needs you to do?

So, let's dive in. What are the next steps you know you need to take? Without overthinking it, focus on what God wants you to do. Now list your top 3 things to do within the next 7 days and add them to your calendar. Include help so you can stay focused and not be busy. If you need to order groceries to be delivered or hire help in other ways - whatever you need to do, add it to the plan because God needs your focus.

I am a creator and I create with God.

The Year of the Creator was written because you are a creator. God designed you for a specific reason. God has a grand vision over your life and you possess something special that only you can bring forth. This means that you possess it now and you do not have to look outside for it, but you must believe and know it. This book is designed to be a tool that helps you tap into God's purpose in your life and release it with God. To free yourself of trying to make things happen. To free yourself from being a starving artist. To free yourself from thoughts that do not define your greatness. To free yourself of frustrations for being a creator, and to step into that God-power inside and create from a space with God, beautifully and in love. By doing this it doesn't free you from hurt or pain but teaches that God equips you.

Say out loud. I am a creator and I create with God. God placed everything I need within me and blessed me with the Holy Spirit to help me navigate this world.

> John 14:26 (KJV) *"But the Helper, the Holy Spirit, whom the Father will send in my name, he will teach you all things and bring to your remembrance all that I have said to you."*

So you're saying to create with God is simple? You just walk with God by being "it", but what if being "it" doesn't look like it should? What does "it" need to look like? Well, you define it. Being "it" is a state of mind. It's knowing GOD has your back, even if you haven't received what you're asking for. God knows what you need, but you'll need to believe and bring it forth by the actions you take with God to create. So, think about, how do you authentically show up. What do you need to have when God opens the door for you?

Bringing forth the creator helps with your confidence and is developed when you show up for what you are asking God for. It's taking the steps to do what it is God is telling you to do. SAY IT OUT LOUD. I am a creator and I am creating with God. The Holy Spirit leads me in the direction I should go. I am listening and I receive it. Amen.

So what does being a creator mean?

According to the Merriam-Webster dictionary Creator" one that <u>creates</u> usually by bringing something new or original into being

Often times people can look at creators as those that are in the art and design world.

Google defines "creator" as:

- God.

- noun: **Creator**; noun: **the Creator**

- And a person or thing that brings something into existence.

However you define creator. Add your name there. You are a creator and you are creative.

I like to break things down in the simplest form to create impact. I know God is the Ultimate Creator and in God, I can create with Him because God gives us the free will to think and create solutions to everyday needs. You choose what you do or do not bring to life. So, you have to ask yourself, "what are you bringing to life each day, through your decisions and what you speak.

Know that you do not have to come up with some new invention or be a designer. Being a creator is part of you naturally if you activate that in your life.

You have to repeatedly strengthen this muscle and continue to step beyond perceived limitations to dream bigger, and to do more Aligned work. I'm not saying at times you won't be busy, but not on nonsense (and that's up to you to know what nonsense is). To embrace being a creator, separate it from being creative. It's not limited to those who create art, however that is a gift from God for someone. At the heart of it, is that we are all creators, so let's get creative.

CHAPTER 2

Designed a Success

You were designed a success. Do not limit your experiences to how you define success. God made you, so, therefore, you are a success.

Think about the following questions and answer them. The answers may evolve throughout changing seasons. The importance is having your core values and knowing who you are and Whose you are. Knowing this will help you know what you stand for.

Remember to be mindful of how you answer the following questions as well. Focus on God's vision for you versus man's and God will reveal what you are to create on his behalf for others.

> Colossians 3:23 (NIV) *"Whatever you do, work at it with all your heart, as working for the Lord, not for human masters."*

- How do I define success?
- What does success look like to me?
- Who am I?
- What do I stand for?

You will be faced with a decision and your character will come through regardless of what you think or who you portray to be. When you peel back all your layers, that's when you see your ultimate belief. You will not be able to keep up with any facades you have created to fit in.

Guess what, you never have to fit in anywhere. God never created you to fit in, but there are people that he wants you to impact through your testimony. So, you must be you. You must be you. You must be you. Again, I ask, who are you?

Take time now to write who you are. Keep it simple. There are no right or wrong answers, but ultimately you are a child of God and God is within you.

Embody what you are creating

You can't control anyone or anything, but yourself. So, you need to show up for yourself right now. It sounds easy but is quite difficult for creators to do.

What do you mean I just have to show up? YES! **(I see one of my advisors in my head, shaking his head yes.)** YOU JUST have to show up with what you have now and add the things you want to see.

Add? How do I add to my current situation? I don't want to be here.

Say you want to move to another place. You are working on the basic things, but you want to see it now.

Think of what you can do to create an oasis in your current space to make you feel confident now as you work towards your move. Find somewhere where you can turn a corner into your space or an area for your goals. Set-up a place to record or a place to create. DO NOT limit yourself, do not look at what you have as not enough. YOU ARE A CREATOR. CREATE WHERE YOU ARE. PERIOD.

Call forth what you need and take aligned steps to start seeing it today. Ok, you see an interesting man or woman on social media and you want to have what they have and be like them. NO! You want to look like you and only do what God built you to do.

You want to present the creator in you. Dress like you, do your makeup and hair like you. Start visiting places you're interested in and participating in activities. Do you! I keep writing "you" because you need to remain you, that is how God will be able to work through you.

He needs the authentic you to create these ideas for sustainability. This will enable you to move in truth and light. Truth in who you are and your light will shine on your creations.

I know. I get it…. Some people seem like they are crushing it. I look at them for inspiration. When jealousy or judgmental thoughts pop up. I say, God, I only want what you want for me. I don't know their story and I'm clear, I only want my life, no one else's.

This comes with practice, of course. Remember, when you are in your flow, you are not worrying about others.

So, it's important to recognize your feelings and identify your "why" in them, to help you move forward.

Success is all around

I've questioned why some are successful and others are not. I've studied patterns and reasons why. I've even questioned at times why others I see are getting opportunities that God knows I want. If I feel myself going to a place where I am hard on myself. I pray for that person and thank God that blessings are right around the corner.

Everyone has a different path. We can look at someone who is successful, but never know the depths of their life and what they have or will experience. We must not try to be like someone else. We must listen to what God has called us to do and focus our feelings on being happy for others.

Success in God

I've felt like a failure when projects weren't successful. However, I know that I am not a failure in God. It's a trick of the enemy to get you to think that you are less than what God created you to be or that your current circumstance is bigger than GOD. Nothing is bigger than God. God designed you with everything inside you to accomplish His will in your life. His will is going to be more amazing than anything you can imagine. I know I keep reiterating that everything is inside you. The sooner you get that in your spirit it will show outwardly in your decisions. You will not look for outside validation.

> Genesis 1:31 (KJV) *"Then God saw everything that He had made, and indeed it was very good."*

What was created was meant to support you in your journey.

Remember when God created the world? On the 7th day, he rested. This is a good example of how to build the ideas inside you. It also shows that any time you call on God, God is already there. So, as you are creating with God, God has already done it for you.

When I was discussing this book with one of my coaches. I planned to get this book out within 3 months. When I asked her if that was realistic, she responded with, "God created the heavens and the earth in 7 days." That response helped remind me of God's power again and to not limit myself.

When you get an idea, you have to dedicate time to it and there needs to be a patient urgency to it. Not an anxious feeling where you are scrambling and making rash decisions. The urgency I'm talking about is when you put in motion the things you know God is telling you to do and remove the insignificant things. It's when you dedicate your time to doing God's will.

When God gives you a book title, thoughts, ideas to make, you must get it out and write it down. In this stage, it doesn't mean that you are pursuing everything. There are conversations with God that you must have, prior. Some ideas are revealed, but for later and some ideas are for you to pursue now.

By taking action on what you hear from God, that is when you will start to get in, be in, and stay in God's flow. Don't worry about getting off track or making the wrong moves. God is there to guide you.

CHAPTER 3

Purpose Acceleration

Surrender

Some people won't ever come around no matter how hard you try. Some people will need to see it before they believe it or you. You must not focus your energy there, you must surrender. Yes, I said must. I don't want to tell you what to do. I'm telling you what I know. God needs your full attention to bring that idea to life. Why? Because it will come with its own set of experiences and now, he is using past experiences and current things to prepare you, so your energy needs to be in God and what he's directing you to do.

So be in tune with things that come up or even people from your past.

I was feeling great today about writing and being productive and two things made me feel different. The first was a trigger from the past hurts. I hadn't felt that way in a while and one conversation caused me to have tension and feel angry. Another was looking at my account and the uneasy feeling of me investing in a company to help me get this book out started to make me question whether this was the right decision. I wondered if I should have waited or if I could have done it and paid a fraction of the cost and used the rest to pay bills.

The feelings you have are legit! That's why it's so important to walk with God. Talk out your feelings with Him and discuss what you are believing Him for. As you take this walk, there will be things that trigger you. There will be things that can cause you to second guess your decision.

Your purpose is to pursue God

Purpose comes up a lot in conversations. There's a need to want to search for it, which can cause different emotions; excitement, frustration, eagerness, fear, etc.

I understand it feels like this grand secret to your life. What if we didn't focus on trying to figure out our purpose? It can be too big and too much to try to focus on, but what if we knew there is purpose in our life and put the focus on pursuing God daily?

We have multiple roles; loved one, friend, professional, sibling, spouse, child, parent and the list goes on. These roles shift in your life at certain times. In each role we play there is a purpose for that role. So instead of boxing ourselves in one area, surrender to God revealing the pieces to your grand purpose.

Focus on your abilities, talents, spiritual gifts, and interests, how you want to show up. What impact you want to have and are having. By shifting your perspective, you shift the atmosphere to flourish in your purpose.

Chapter 4

Say Yes

SWAY Passions

Sway Passions is a term I coined which stands for "Start with a Yes" (SWAY)! Meaning start with permitting yourself to go after your goals instead of swaying back and forth and never moving beyond the idea. We often hold ourselves in bondage to things that don't matter or that someone else put on us. When we are free in God. Once you give yourself permission, it's time to focus on the one thing you will start. You do this by deciding what you're interested in, what it will take to get it started, what the return potential is and what you are hearing God tell you to pursue. It may not be a project, program, or business. It may be forgiveness, cleaning, organizing, etc in this season. Get this in order before you embark on this grand God-goal so that you can remove what could hinder you.

Do your best not to get caught up in an idea overload and think that you must pursue all of them. Know that ideas intertwine and you'll be surprised at how your many talents will mesh once you get started with one idea.

Do not pursue something because you solely want to be like someone else. There is a purpose in your life and God wants you to bring it forward. It's to help you get clear now, this is a journey with God.

Some questions to consider are:

Who are you?

What is your why?

Do you believe GOD is right there with you? IF YES….. if no? Why

Do you know God is with you? IF YES….. if no? Why

DIDN'T you just ask me this question… yes! But in a different way. See, you have to believe it and you have to know it. There will be ebbs and flow in your life but what will be constant is God's LOVE for you and his wanting for you to do the things you were meant to do in life.

> Joshua 1:9 NIV *"Have I not commanded you? Be strong and courageous; do not be frightened or dismayed, for the Lord your God is with you wherever you go."*

GOD-FIDENCE

Once you SWAY in God, you will no longer only go side to side, You will be in Gods flow. You will show up differently and more confidently.

Have you heard someone tell you to just be you or to embody what you are seeking? Is that easy or challenging for you? Do you find yourself doing it at times and then going back to habits? It's easy to overcomplicate this and to keep from moving forward. I find through conversations with creators having confidence is what is holding them back from pursuing their goals.

I get it. There are things I'm having to do that I don't feel confident in, but I have to do them anyway. In doing them I continue to build confidence internally through knowledge and repetition. I also have to show up in power and change my conversation of being confident off of me and place my confidence in God, by knowing that God will not fail me. That is the secret weapon. It's one thing to fake confidence, but that does not last. Walk boldly in our GOD-fidence.

Think big and know that God is moving in ways that you can't even imagine. You will encounter disbelief, but it's the lens you see it through. Are you seeing the lack and smallness around you? If so, recognize that, but do not accept that into your space, into your mind. Think big. Now think bigger and step out on faith

There is no way GOD, THE ULTIMATE CREATOR, would limit your abilities and keep you in small places, no way. However, there is a lesson and a reason for this season. Know that each season is your season just like each year is your year and in the hands of the creator. Each year is the year of the creator and even if you don't create your God-given ideas and solutions you will still be creating. You might as well tap into the abundance that is already inside you and stop trying to do it alone, without God. God designed you and holds the instructions.

Chapter 5

PERSPECTIVE SHIFT

In the middle, will check your authenticity

Perspective is everything. When you feel a sense of frustration, do your best to shift that lens to God and know that all is well and all is working out for your good.

Things you declare or say you want will go through a process of determining it's authenticity. There have been times when I asked God why he would allow me to go through that when I know the vision was from Him and I'm a good person. Being a good person is great, but it doesn't eliminate you. Jesus was a great person. So, you know that you will go through life and God will always bring you the victory.

I have to be mindful of feeling that way because it is a way to start doubting God's word. I have some great people in my reach that remind me of God's favor. There are things we will go through (some things we brought on ourselves because God gives us free will) so that we develop the tools and wisdom for the next step God is bringing us to.

I'm writing this at a place in my life where I'm in the middle. This time is imperative for my next season, or I will find myself repeating where I'm at now.

It reminds me of when Jonah was supposed to go to Nineveh but instead headed to Tarshish. He headed there by boat through Joppa. Joppa was significant because it was the place in between, the place in the middle.

In the middle is where you can turn either way. In the middle is where you can reset and pivot. In the middle is where you can find clarity on where you are being led by God. Did you get let go of a job (God released you to your dreams)? Did a deal fall through (God has better plans for you)? Did you lose something important (God will give you back what you lost and more)? Are you in-between decisions (God is sending you the answer or it's already there)?

Resist looking at the middle as a hindrance or where you are lost. Resist trying to escape. Embrace this middle place for you to fulfill God's purpose.

Leaping over Barriers

I talked with, let's say his name is John, and when asked about how he communicates with God and if he does things with God. He responded, "I believe in God and I'm living my life and handling what comes up". I then proceeded with asking "do you consult with God or ask what your next direction should be?" John's response was "no, I'm not waiting and sitting down listening for God to tell me what to do. This seems like wu-wu stuff and not realistic. God says work and I'm working."

He gave me the weirdest look and I got it. This approach can be taken as you are waiting and not moving, but sitting and listening for lightning to strike and the clouds to descend and this thunderous voice to say "_____ (fill in your name] Go this route now!" I don't make God spooky. I don't make God hard in my life. When I say God spoke to me, it's an inner voice beyond feelings. It's from a daily (throughout the day) practice of talking to God and listening.

This will develop into a spiritual intuition. We all experience it, it's an inner guide and knowing. Based on who you talk to, intuition and the

Holy Spirit are not the same. I don't know this answer, but I look at them as intertwined and connected. People could try to argue that my gut reaction is based on logic, but I look at it as an inner knowing with a deeper understanding and connection to the decision.

So, I asked John, the intuition you have to work and to just do, have you thought of that being part of what God wants you to be doing and if so, are there questions you can ask God during that time on aligned moves you can make instead. It's worth it to try. God's already seen the outcome of what you are doing. God also has some great moves you can make in the process to the greater He has in your life and could make your day more efficient so you don't just have to be in worker mode.

I don't know if he tried it, but I hope that he did. It's interesting how we can get caught in the rut of life, which becomes hard to get out of when we are just doing, but if we stop to ask God questions, this is a strategy all on its own. It's not selfish or mischievous. It's also not a burden. God wants us to co-create with him this vision. God needs you to fulfill it to glorify His name and to show more people His power.

> Isaiah 65:24 (NIV) *"Before they call I will answer; while they are still speaking I will hear."*

Feelings in check

This bible verse helps me check into my feelings with direction.

> Philippians 4:6-7 (NIV) *"Do not be anxious about anything, but in every situation, by prayer and petition, with thanksgiving, present your requests to God. And the peace of God, which transcends all understanding, will guard your hearts and your minds in Christ Jesus."*

I had to often check in on my emotions when writing this book. I know you will see me, but more than that I want this book to be a tool in your toolbox. Things are going on in my life, as I write now the hives on my body are starting to flare up again and itch to where it's uncomfortable, but writing this book excites me and takes my mind off of it for the moment. When I'm creating I bring an excited energy to building. I know the difference when I give something my all versus rushing it or when I did it for reasons other than a higher purpose.

Think about the feelings you're experiencing and give them to God.

Chapter 6

Plan

Plan it, but move in it

Having a plan helps activate your next steps and set a course of action. God wants you to plan and share that plan. There are resources all around you that God wants to connect you with. There's someone's purpose tied to you showing up. Once you encounter these resources it's important to be ready and to be able to explain it to them, so they get it and can do their part.

> Habakkuk 2:2 (KJV) *"Write the vision And make it plain on tablets, That he may run who reads it."*

Write the plan. Write the vision.

If you want to write a book. What's your plan to writing it, but also getting it in the hands of people who need to read it?

Having a plan also helps you stay focused and anything that doesn't align with it, you are less likely to do it because you want to stay on track with your goals.

Also, take into account your responsibilities and how much time you will need for your action steps.

It's time to plan. This plan is needed, but it will be a plan that you allow God to write and edit.

Identify how much time you have and the days you can commit to the plan. It is a must that you believe in it so that you will do it. It has to be non-negotiable. Yes, things come up or maybe days where you're tired or sick. Think about things you can put into place like an app for voice recording your thoughts or you have a loved-one on standby to help you with the kids. Know that you are not in this by yourself. On days where you need to take off and rest in God do that to rejuvenate. The key is to start again and to not give up

Incorporate a daily check-in. So that by the end of each year you don't look around like what the bleep just happened. Where did my time go? If you want by the end of the year to have accomplished your God-goals. It's a must to be intentional and move with GOD.

This is not about doing, doing, doing. Be it!

There was a time when I didn't focus on the knowledge I had. I was looking for another outlet (searching for the secret to success) and I signed up for an entrepreneurship training program. I stayed in it for 2 years and spent my savings doing it.

It was an expensive way for me to realize that I already had the tools inside me and no one could help me until I was clear on my goals, products, and services. There were many things I didn't know like building a funnel or setting up a landing page, but Google also has that info. I didn't realize that everything was within me that I needed and the training I was receiving was to build confidence. It was a high price to pay, but it's part of my journey and I can't dwell on it. I met some amazing people and God worked it out for other blessings to be within that experience. I wouldn't change that experience. It has helped me be a better leader and sharpened my skills.

Take note, you should seek to educate yourself, but if you do fill yourself up with more knowledge, determine what is necessary. If you want to be a doctor, then higher education is required. If you want to be an entrepreneur, yes...go to school and or attend training. Also know having a coach or mentor is important. Just know in addition to learning is implementation, and also showing up and pulling out what you already possess. Overall you have what you need right now to get started. Watch what you're investing in and wasting time and money on. FOMO (fear of missing out) will have you searching for it on the hunt for the next thing. When in reality you have what you need for your next steps.

You utilize tools to bring forth God's vision, not be the tool.

This is not about working all the time and toiling away. Yes, work is required but remember you are God's child, not God's employee. There is a big difference in this mindset because it will determine how you show-up, versus knowing you have the benefits and working in them, versus toiling away trying to get something that is already your birthright.

It will not be easy breezy all the time either, but there is a grace and ease within God.

You're going to be creating late at night or early morning or throughout the day. You're going to have sacrifices. You're going to be faced with something not working. You're going to be faced with deadlines. So talk to God for strategies of what to do in these times.

Sacrifice

Belief, dedication, and action are keys to seeing your GOD-goal become reality.

So what are you dedicated to doing? What are you willing to and not willing to sacrifice?

I believe God will provide us with an abundant life. SO as we are pursuing these goals, be mindful of the other areas that are also within your purpose and are a blessing. You do not have to have one or the other. You can have a successful career and family.

I will not wake up one day and my kids do not want to be around me because they didn't feel like I loved them, so that means that I have to be present with them now. I say them, because hey God may have more children for me in the future. I currently have a 7-year-old and it can be challenging trying to work around him because of course he wants to always play.

So, I have to carve out times for him my husband and time for me to create. Some days are more progressive than others, some days I work more, but I always hug him and tell him what's going on, some days we play and most of the time we are together. The importance is that I'm there and he sees me creating ideas and hears me talking about God and praying. He also first-hand witnesses my reaction to failures and success.

My prayers are that it is positively impactful on him. He already thinks he can create whatever and has zero fears. He often tells me, Mom, It's time to turn off your brain (then he will have me lean in and he pretends that he is unscrewing my brain as if to turn it off.) Once complete then he says, "let go" and I immediately pretend to let go, not think about it and jump. Today I dove into his slip and slide (ouch! I hit my toes when I did it, but anyway) the point is to know there is a grand purpose and to define what is important to you and carve out time for it. This is my life, determine what is important to you. If something wasn't a priority, you can start today by prioritizing it. Do not beat yourself up.

I have to tell you things while it's happening. As I write this I am refusing to get on Facebook. Several times I have picked up my phone to scroll online, but I keep hearing no, stay in the flow. So put down whatever distractions are keeping you from releasing that idea and stay in the flow.)

Keep going. Read insightful books like this and listen to podcasts that will serve you in the flow and not stop your flow.

What are the things you can do to get started after you discuss this plan with God?

Look at your goal and write down steps it will take to get there. Then get clear on the most important things that you can do to get there. Clean, organize, complete the paperwork, finish the degree, sign-up for the program, ask, write the proposal, make it, hire.

I'll stop there... there are things you can do. You have to take the initiative to do what is in your power and then literally let it go from there. You can check-in, follow the guidelines and requirements, but then let it go. Don't manipulate it, don't try to make someone participate, and don't try to hold on to someone. When you've done what you can do. You gotta let go and stay in God's presence.

When you've done what you can do. Stay in the presence of God by communicating daily for your next steps and continue to handle your responsibilities and dream with God. God wants to take you further than you can imagine.

Chapter 7

The Power of Praying and Fasting

Prayer

Prayer is you talking to God. Thanking God and asking for guidance and direction. Fasting is you listening to God in a way that gets to the heart of it because at that time you are giving up food that actually has power over your flesh to focus on what God is saying to you. There are things over our life that if we are not careful can have power over us. It's important on your journey with God that you fast and pray to clear out the clutter and hear from God. When you do this you will experience even greater changes after the fast on what you eat and partake in. Talk to God on how often and when he wants you to fast.

When you hear God..... Move

It can be interesting how you will hear from GOD. There are times when I do not want to work on a goal like before I started writing this section. One morning, I woke up at 7:35am to get some water and I could barely keep my eyes open. I couldn't wait to get back in the bed, and when I returned to the bed I realized my scarf was off and if anyone knows, hair, especially my type of hair you immediately put your scarf on to avoid drying it out.

Well, I found my scarf, which made me wake up more and by the time my head hit the pillow God was sending me words to write in this book. God kept replaying and adding new words in my head and all I could think was that's good, but I really want to sleep, I'm not tired, but the BED feels so good.

My husband and son are still asleep, which actually makes this the perfect time, so I drag myself out of bed while trying to find a voice recording option, that took about 15 minutes and everything in my spirit said to just begin writing, well I'm writing and it's flowing. It's 8:16 am and I hear the alarm on my husband's phone go off, I continue to write in hopes that I will get to write at least until 9 am.

I could have stayed in bed and not wrote, but when God tells you to move, it's important to move.

I will make it non-negotiable that I will write at any time to get this book written. I must get it out of me, just like God has an idea for you that he built into you.

I believe and know that self-sabotage is a reason for goals not being a reality. I say know. I didn't pull data for it, but because of my background in event planning, case management and research. I have been surveying individuals old and young, since I was a teenager. Those I met along the way in nursing homes and hospitals and VIP's of my family and others that I have studied online. Some were conversations and others observations. Sometimes I was able to hear about their past stories and unfulfilled dreams. Beware of self-sabotage. Where you do things that keep you from your God-goals.

Talk to God

If in 2018, God would have spoken to me, and said… Well, first let me explain what I mean when I say "God spoke".

When I say that God spoke to me, I am not saying that I saw God and we had this conversation. I'm saying that God reveals his will in your life through time with him, through reading the bible and listening to spirit led content, it's an inner knowing. It's not just a feeling because feelings can be deceiving.

My feelings right now would tell me I want a dessert, however that dessert doesn't support my weight loss goals. Don't just go by a feeling. Ask God questions and listen for the answers you hear and are shown. Talking to God has to be practiced.

What do you think God has been telling you to do?

Do not discount the things you do that appear small or insignificant.

Zechariah 4:10 (NLT) says, "*Do not despise these small beginnings, for the LORD rejoices to see the work begin.*"

Write them all down, do not edit, do not judge, do not ask anyone else what they think. This is between you and God. He needs to work something out in you before you muddy it up with others' opinions.

God needs you to be in his presence and power to get you to your next step. Pray over clarity, pray over an understanding of what to do and what to pursue. Pray until you get an answer.

Jeremiah 29:13 (NIV), "*You will seek me and find me when you seek me with all your heart.*"

What if I don't get an answer? You will get an answer. It's just if you listen or not and whether you do it or not. For a long time, all I heard was to clean and to organize. Yes, I still did daily tasks, cooked, and worked my day job, but I had to prioritize cleaning my desk and going through paperwork. As much as I wanted to speak on stages, write books, and do photoshoots.

All the fun things. That was not the season for it. Organizing my files and purging items in my home to make room was a priority. I stayed in this season for months because I kept prioritizing other opportunities when only that kept delaying my next step with God.

God will not reveal everything to you, but the instructions you receive will help set you up for your God-goal and if you don't do it, you will notice that you are still in the same place and are not ready when the opportunities come.

Let me return back to, "If in 2018".

If in 2018, God would have told me that you will produce the most beautiful show. I will use you as an example to show others that I'm in them to create, the show will be a strong representation of all people coming together, it will be part of your legacy, but to do so, I will not allow others to invest in it fully. I need you to know my power and I need you to experience a few things that will develop your wisdom for future places that I am taking you. You will feel like I forgot you, like your idea paid everyone else but you, you will focus on money because as a result of the show and me not allowing other funders you will have to pay for the show with the money I send you through working a day job.

In that process, you will be let go from your job and you will feel even more pressure after it. Due to emotions and stress you will start experiencing swelling and hives. It will be uncomfortable, you will have tension in your home because of your attitude… and feel thoughts of lack and jealousy, which will make you feel insecure.

If God would have told me what would happen after the show. I still would have pursued it, because it's true to my purpose and I would do it over in a heartbeat.

I had to get to the root of my worries and feelings. I had to release pressures that I put on myself and do it with God. I had to daily, often hourly, remind myself that God is with me and to start with a simple plan to start moving forward.

Listen to God

You always get an answer. It just may not be the answer you seek.

After the show, the answers I wanted was how to make the money back, but with every try, I didn't get the answer I was seeking. The money that did come I used towards it. I had to pray for mindset shifts and strength, the only answers I received were to clean up, get back to the basics. I also heard to write a book, but it was a thought that I couldn't even start on because I needed to clean internally and in my environments. I looked at all my bills and canceled what I didn't need, I went through my supplies and home and cleaned. It took me months to do, but what I learned is cleaning is a constant part of this process. 1 year later and I'm back to this yearning of cleaning, organizing and also creating. This will never end, so it's important to listen, because that knowledge is the insight to future activities that need us to do what is current to receive the blessings then. So, I'm adopting purging and cleaning to every season.

Are you listening?

What are you hearing to do? I can't answer this question for you... no one can. NOT A COACH, NOT A PARENT.... NO ONE.... NO ONE.... NO ONE..... God blesses you with others who aid in fulfilling God's purpose. When you find these individuals remember they are not your answer, they are a vessel and you also check-in with God first, during, and after, don't turn this person into your savior.

Or it will be easy for you to get off track and start embarking on a journey and ideas that are not yours to pursue. If you find yourself in that space, DO NOT beat yourself up, know that God is in you for immediate shifts and he creates openings for you to pivot back to what he is calling you to do.

Prayer aka talking to God is your lifeline. It's an essential part of this journey to being the creator God called you to be.

Again, it is easier said than done, but when you feel emotions it's important to check in, don't let lack, fear, doubt, _____ (you fill in the blank) keep you from pursuing that God-goal.

REMEMBER that doubt is a distraction keeping you from bringing forth that idea. It can cause you to continue to play small.

You can evaluate each idea and be conscious of things that occur within it. There are ideas that I pursued that served me in a particular season for God to reveal the truth to me, but once that was over, everything within me said to flee and I did. At times where I hesitated, it was an uneasy feeling inside me where I knew this was not the right move. I've learned that if I don't make the decision, God will.

What I don't want this book to be is fluff. Telling you, that you can do anything you set your mind to do and that every time it will be successful.

What I have learned is when you keep God's presence in your life, you can expect greatness and success.

Chapter 8

Where to Start

Words have Power

Start with being open to doing things God's way and begin to pray. These prayers can be any length you choose, the point is to begin talking to God. I find it very helpful to find bible verses that I can add to my prayers to help me calm my mind and focus on the word. Words have power and whether we say positive or negative things, there is an outcome produced by the words we use and the words we internalize that others have said to us. It's great to include scriptures as a reference to God's promises. Here's an example of a prayer using scripture:

Dear Heavenly Father,

I ask you to clear my mind of thoughts not helping me in this stage. You know the desires you placed on my heart and how I want to fulfill your vision in my life. I know that my words have your power, John 1:1 (NIV) states, "In the beginning was the Word, and the Word was with God, and the Word was God". So I know that the words I speak are powerful and shift the atmosphere. I know that you will position me to accomplish this vision. I ask for clarity on my next steps and where you want me to concentrate on. Thank you for your guidance, I receive it in Jesus name.

What is my next aligned step?

What do you think about the options you have? This is a question that only God can reveal to you. What do you clearly hear if you remove any doubts? One great way is to look at your past and think about what you don't want to do or don't want in your life and be crystal clear on that.

Next focus on your past adventures and projects. What lit you up? What did you want to do, but never tried? What would you do no matter what? This will be the start of you deciding your next steps with God.

Finding the Motivation to Keep Going

I've spent a lot of time observing people and listening to stories on why they did or did not go after their dreams.

I know for me, it's not fear. Sometimes fear tries to creep in to put a damper on my excitement. I think about death and not getting out what God needs me to release, but I have no problems talking about death. I care more about making sure my son is set up with the tools and resources he needs than I fear death. I am dedicated to releasing my God-given ideas because for me it's a must to do. I don't want to live my life not accomplishing what I was born to accomplish.

What is your motivation?

Called to Create

For the longest time, I only heard to clean up, to get ready. I still hear that and know that should be ongoing, but more than ever I hear to create. It's a beautiful thing to be able to do.

Everything in my spirit tells me that writing this book is the right move, yet so many distractions are coming my way. I have to continue to refocus daily so that I get this out with God.

You were called to create. This is about your journey with God and knowing that God placed inside you desires that only you were created to accomplish. Now how do we accomplish these ideas? Yes, there's strategy. Yes, there are connections.

Yes, resources are needed. However above all there is a manual and guess what? The manual is located inside you. The manual is God and God is right there with you and will provide, but he needs you to make the decision and put forth the action.

I don't know if you are reading this, and saying *but* in your head.

- But how will I do it
- But how will I pay for it
- But will they support me
- But when will I get the time
- But do you know how much money I have in my account

But BUT BUT but…. SAY NO to any buts. Those are limiting beliefs and you are creating with the Ultimate Creator.

Say yes and surrender. At times, this will feel hard, it may even feel like you do not know if God is there. If you ever feel that way, say God I don't feel you, but I know you're there, show me the way. Acknowledge God's presence always. Distractions and lies will be lurking around and it's important for you to stay in God's presence, by asking for guidance and showing gratitude.

The presence of God can take place in your heart, you do not need the right environment, you can call on God and He will hear you.

Utilize What You Have

Ask God what is in your possession now to use.

Focus on what you can do today and at any time when you need rest, get rest.

Do your best to break tasks into the most simplistic next steps and strategies. Yes, you want more, but what do you currently have to move the needle forward and get started.

> 2 Kings 4:1-7 (NLV) Elisha said to her, *"What can I do for you? Tell me, what do you have in the house?"* And she said, *"Your woman servant has nothing in the house except a jar of oil."* Then he said, *"Go around and get jars from all your neighbors. Get empty jars, many of them. Then go in and shut the door behind you and your sons. Pour the oil into all these jars, and set aside each one that is full."* So she went from him and shut the door behind her and her sons. They took the jars to her, and she poured. When the jars were full, she said to her son, *"Bring me another jar."* And he said to her, *"There is not one jar left."* Then the oil stopped flowing. She came and told the man of God. And he said, *"Go and sell the oil and pay what you owe. You and your sons can live on the rest."*

The passage shows community, faithfulness, legacy building and God's love. Continue to put your faith in God and watch God turn what you think is small into more impact and abundance. God's vision for us is beyond what we can imagine.

Let's get excited, start where we can and continue to show-up!

Chapter 9

Faith in the Midst

F- It (FAITH IT)

God's timing is not our timing. Have faith in the midst. God blessed us with seasons and timeframes to help us break down the things He wanted us to accomplish. This helps us frame our years and helps us see progress. God doesn't live in time with us.

You embody what you are asking God for and you create with God… not step in front of Him, not try to go the backdoor route, not try to leave God out, but in every decision make it a must to talk to God. He is your life's mentor, Creator, and He sees every piece of the puzzle of your life. I believe that because God gives us the power of free will. Our decisions have different outcomes, but in the end, He always brings us back to Him, so it's important what you take on and how you handle what you are pursuing. Whether or not you consciously know it, every decision you make is leading you somewhere.

I'm doing it. Where's the abundance?

Check-in with your intentions. Keep your eye on God and do not make the goal more important than God.

It's interesting because there have been ideas that I knew God was in. I just know it still. Yet the abundance that I thought would occur, didn't and it resulted in me having to carry burdens and a big sacrifice on me personally. There have been people that I just knew God wanted me to bless and serve them from a place of helping their ideas, but in the end they treated me in unfavorable ways or had ulterior motives. I wondered why God would allow me to be in those places and to experience that.

After getting out of my feelings a friend had to remind me that God is not done and God is not in my timing. So those projects and people were seeds and those seeds are growing and one day they will be ready for harvest. The decisions of my past, God is working that out for my good today and in the future. So, I cannot look at that as a loss, only as a gain. It was definitely a gain in knowledge. There are some things I will never do again and I know that it was a set-up for greater impact. There are some things that I will keep pursuing because there is a higher purpose in it.

Like me producing Indiana Fashion Week. Indiana Fashion Week turned out beautiful, amazing, GOD'S spirit was all through it. It brought many people together through the love of fashion but the result of not getting fully funded resulted in me having to pay for the expense, which challenged everything in me. I was conflicted because if I pay out of my pocket am I trying to take over it and not allow God to send me the money.

At some point, I had to stop going back and forth in my mind about what God wanted me to do. My feelings were too heavily wrapped in it, so at times the discussion in my head was unclear, but what was clear is that God was on it and God blessed me with my current income flow from my day job, Which also made it harder because my day job was ending by the end of the year (December 2019).

I spent 9 months feeling down and sad. I can say that now because I can see clearer now. During that time, I continued to create through it and clean, go through paperwork, clean my office, my home, and just get organized. Which was the only direction I know God gave me permission to do, as much as I wanted to get booked for jobs or create a product line. The only thing I felt heavy about was cleaning. I was heartbroken and this wasn't the first idea that did not return the funds needed to continue.

Through the crying I continued to do what I could. I was working a full-time job. I would take the majority of my check and pay off the show balance. I felt like a failure and I hated taking money away that could be used personally or saved.

18 months later and it was paid off. I prayed for God to send the resource and some did come. I know if God wanted to he could have paid it already or could pay it today, so there is a lesson in this season of my life.

I made it a point to have a cheerful heart around money, because again it is all God's. I also realized I was placing my worth and measure of success on money. Primarily because I just don't want to put my family in jeopardy for my dreams. Even though I feel called to do it, I have to use discernment. My family is also my purpose and they have to be taken care of too.

When I would take the money that God blessed me with to pay off the show bills, I felt so conflicted, why would God give me these ideas. I know one thousand percent it was his grace and direction to pursue it, but why was this bill left for me to pay it. I understand there's sacrifice, but it's been 20 years.

Everyone else received value, many received payment, but I was left with what I thought would be overflow for me to generate income to live and also to have money to put into the next fashion project to ultimately help others succeed. I asked God several questions and oftentimes didn't receive the answers that I wanted. I still don't have an answer. Other than God is not done and he needed to put me in a position and that was required at that time to bring forth His vision.

I share this with you because it is a lesson to help you see that when you're creating things may not turn out how you expect, but expect God to work and hold on to that thought always. Especially in times when you pursue your God-given goals and the results do not look like you thought they would.

I do not share this to scare you or cause you to question your next steps. I say expect God to work because everything works out in your favor. Everything! Even if it doesn't seem like it now. Your story is still being written every day. God is always on time.

Watch Out for the "They"

If you are still waiting to see it, steer clear from They. Who are they? They is whoever or whatever information that is opposite of what God told you! What God promised you! What God made you for!

They this and they that. I'm not going to spend much time on this topic. Worrying about they will keep you from fulfilling God's purpose. They will tell you that you can't do it. They will tell you that you will never be healed. They will tell you that it is over. Limitations will always be placed on things and you, so you have to realize what that is, but more importantly whose you are and keep persevering.

Embody it

Embody what you seek. When doing this it will repel and also attract.

Some people you encounter will not understand you, they may say you've changed. That is okay. You will evolve when you really realize how much God loves you and that you are designed for greatness.

You will no longer do some of your past things or hang with some of the people you used to. You will commit to the pursuit of fulfilling what God has for you. Know that in times you are weary God will sustain you. Isaiah 46:4 (AMP) *"Even to your old age I am He, And even to your advanced old age I will carry you! I have made you, and I will carry you; Be assured I will carry you and I will save you."*

Take each step in God and when you do encounter opposition, stand strong and confident in God. I don't say this lightly. I say it to you as I have said it to myself through racism, sexism, failed "me" led project (where I stepped ahead of God), hurt, the murder of my cousin, and experiencing swelling for the last 300 plus days and the doctor saying there's nothing they can do for me but give me medication and the symptoms might not go away.

Let nothing deter you from creating what God has given you. There will never be a right time. Consider today being the day you get it out of your head and make a commitment with God to pursue it. When you make that commitment, it's a daily walk. So, begin to experience it through the actions you take. Ask yourself daily, does this align with God's plans for me? Embody it!

Chapter 10

Creating Resources and Opportunities

Money Money Money

Notice around you how decisions are made. Was money a final decision? Everything comes down to money. What you do. Where you go. What you pursue or don't pursue. Based on your thoughts about money it will be the driving factor to your decisions. God will place an idea for you to pursue, not always though, will God reveal the resources for it.

What decision have you made in the past based on money? The beliefs and resources you currently have can factor into your next steps. Instead, it should be the opposite. We should believe God for the vision and step out on faith no matter what resources are present.

All the money is here on earth. It has not left. God possesses it all along with the answers to the ways He will bless us. I know we can look around at others and see their blessings and wonder why God gave them all of that and you so little or what seems like not the abundance you seek. Focus on the good. Focus on God. God sees you.

> Matthew 6:33 (ESV) *"But seek first the kingdom of God and his righteousness, and all these things will be added to you."*

The ideas and plans God wants you to create will generate income and build legacy. With God, you will create money flow. You got to believe and know this. You will have impact and profit. There is nothing wrong with serving others and making money.

Take some time now to journal your feelings about money?

What are the first words that pop into your head about money?

Are you willing to trust that you can pursue your God goal without having all the resources currently? Don't let anyone tell you there's no money, people aren't spending money, or you'll never make money. The truth is that the money is here and again someone has it. We just have to unlock it.

Answer honestly, as you are pursuing this goal. The money topic is going to come up all the time. Don't run from it. Don't be afraid of money. You are not selfish for wanting money. You are not wrong for wanting money. Get comfortable with money being a tool. Get comfortable receiving money because if you want to make an impact you will be able to use that money to create great rippling effects in the world as a creator, creating with God. The resources are going to come and guess what sometimes it is not going to be in the form of currency.

It can be in a person or an experience, like for instance, You are wanting the money to produce an event, but instead of money, you receive an opportunity to use a facility at 50% off. Well, that's money that you don't have to pay for the place. Be open to all the blessings you will receive, when you are aware of money, open to receiving it and keep God first, God will provide.

Like everything else, this is something you continue to put in practice. For a decade I saved money and within the last 3 years, I used all the money on education, business ideas, workshops, and masterminds. Being unemployed, that money would be helpful now, so at times I'm down on myself for my decisions. I hold on to knowing that I made the right decision in that season and now, it's time to show up in a way that embodies what I'm pursuing now. Plus spending that money was me investing in my purpose.

What are you holding on to from the past that's keeping you from moving forward?

What did you learn from it?

What do you want now?

Repeat this.

My past was a stepping stone to my future. God is with me and making each new day better than the last. I will boldly move forward in my God-given goals. Everything will be restored abundantly to me. I will walk in faith and not by sight. I will pursue _____ (fill in the blank with your God-goal). The resources are there and God will use people and opportunities to bless you right on time.

It will cost either way.

One thing I've learned is that it will cost you something. It will cost you time, money and energy. The thing is, God blesses you with others who can help you bring your ideas to life, and like you, they also should get paid.

I hired a team to help me get this book out. This is part of the flow. If I DIY this book, I'm clear I would be blocking God's next assignment for me. I would stay in the wilderness, roaming, feeling stuck, pushing back this God-goal when I know I'm meant to complete "Year of the Creator" in this season. I'd also see that I'm not stuck. I'm just not in action on the right things for me. I'm not opening up to God to get out of the wilderness. I'm stuck because I choose to be stuck.

So whether you release your ideas or not, it will cost you or maybe even your future generation something.

What do you have to lose?

Support

Know who's who….. People are going to come in and out of your life. They will give you advice and have their own beliefs and motives. Be open to people who want to create with you to help bring forth the vision. Just use discernment and do your best to not let them deter you from what God is telling you.

You will also have others who will say that God spoke a word in your life and this is what He told me to tell you to do. I believe that God gives us all gifts and someone may have a word for you, just check their word with God's word to you directly.

Do not make a move without talking to God first. If you feel yourself putting someone else's opinions in front of God's word to you: Stop! Get quiet and regroup. Don't put anything or anyone in front of God.

Why because again this can lead you down paths that were not for you.

I know within the God-goals I've had, I've made purchases that I should have not purchased and the list goes on in life when it comes to investments and projects I took on. We're not going to stop here to rehash what we should have or could have done. We'll utilize that as a lesson and not one to scare us from moving forward but to propel us in wisdom for our future projects.

You also have those that you LOVE and who love you, but they don't get what you are doing, and they may not even support you. Release them and pray to God what you want from them, but release them. God's got some other people He wants to connect you with, but first, you have to create it! What's it? Only you have the answers. So start by being what you seek.

Know that who loves you will support you in the capacity that they understand and know. God is also working on them, so show them grace. My husband works a lot to provide for us. He dreams, but he's realistic.

HE REALIZES things he wants to change, but he focuses a lot on what must be taken care of now so that we are taken care of.

I understand this about him. He knows I'm a dreamer, he knows I will take action. He knows that when I set my mind on something I will do it. I understand that not all my dreams have brought a monetary return to the family and some strains are placed when the other source of income is not bringing in money, but spending it. He has encouraged me to continue, but to continue to use wisdom. For that, I both respect and honor him.

There's also the family who won't support you or who are negative. You have to know what conversations to have and what questions to quickly exit when around them. You do not have to prove yourself or your ideas and you do not need permission. GOD already gave it to you….. Let that sink in.

You have everything you need right now in the season you are in to make your next move, because again, whether you intentionally make a move or not, remember even if you don't move, you are still moving. Things are moving around you. Things are changing and whether you consciously make a stance to change you are still changing as well as the environment.

The Right opportunity vs. the Aligned opportunity for me

Just like creating money, when you're in action, you will create opportunities.

This is why it's very important to build the relationship of talking to God, so you can decipher the opportunities coming your way and which to pursue.

You want to be able to identify which are wrong and out of alignment and which are good opportunities, but not good for you. And you want to be able to walk confidently into the opportunities that are good and right for you.

There is discernment between a good opportunity and an aligned opportunity.

This week alone, I was approached to do one project that would take about 30 hours of my time along with an approach to sell a weight loss product, both seemed like good opportunities and could lead to building revenue and networking; however, they both are not aligned with the 2 goals I know I'm supposed to pursue in this season. As I was thinking about what to do, I knew it was a no. I started feeling FOMO (fear of missing out) and this anxious feeling which is an indication to me that I am out of alignment. I must finish my current assignments.

It's easy to get overwhelmed, thinking you will choose the wrong one. Remember, God connects each experience you have to your overall purpose and benefit. Pray for direction.

Chapter 11

God's Plan for You is Bigger

My objective is to help you get started or to move forward. Don't try to out think God by overthinking. Just dream, plan, and take action.

As you plan it's a good idea to project goals and develop a timeline, but I don't want you to get stuck in a dream world where you don't take the necessary steps. We all know that life evolves each day, but we do have the ability to shape it based on our thoughts, beliefs, and actions.

Take time to dream and think of what you want to accomplish in the time frames below. It's important to plan for the future and ask yourself would your past self be proud of you. Are you saving money for a down payment on a house? Did you take the exam? Are you moving forward with an idea?

You are only promised right now and right now is a good time to enjoy life and plan for the amazing future God has planned for you.

Take 15 minutes on each section and write the answers to the following:

Where are you at in your career?

How do you want to feel, regarding where you are at in this stage?

What do you want to add to your look?

Are there any changes in your current environment that you need to make?

Who's with you and are they adding or deterring you from your goals?

What have you accomplished?

What's your financial status?

What impact have you made?

What are you proud of?

Feel free to add more questions. Come back to these questions quarterly and use them as a guide to check-in with yourself. By asking yourself questions it will be a guide to your prayers each day.

Think about the last 30 days and how creativity showed up in your life.

Don't make this hard. The simplest things can be creative (which makes you a creator).

Are you working from home and had to stack a bunch of books up to level your computer and then organize the section behind you?

Are you now homeschooling your kid(s) and having to come up with activities? These are creative ways we show up in our everyday life.

If you are a cook, are you finding ways to remake that hamburger, spaghetti, salad…….

I can go on and on, but think about personally in your home, how you have been creative?

This can seem like it doesn't matter, but it does. You must realize you are both creative and a creator.

If you think about it. You'll start to notice how creative you are and not disregard it.

NOW:

So, we've talked about why and we've briefly looked into the future (because now is what you have). You've reflected on ways to get started. You have committed to bringing forth your God-given goal. If not, this book Year of the Creator, will be where you left it when you are ready. I pray you move forward with your goals.

Let God know that you will follow Him and bring forth that idea. Let God know your feelings. God already knows, but by expressing them it may help you to feel heard and seen (if that is something you desire). It can also be comforting knowing that God is right there.

So how do you create with God, the Ultimate Creator? One way is through your natural abilities because you were made in His image.

> Genesis 1:27 (ESV), "So God created man in His own image; in the image of God He created him; male and female He created them."

This book is interesting to be released at this time because I could have continued to hold onto it, procrastinate, and not organize my thoughts. Instead, I chose to align my plans with God's plans for me and bring them forth. I've had several years of experiencing the power of bringing ideas to life. Whether it was God-ordained or not.

I've experienced releasing a project and having success and failures. I share this because I want to show that it's not one destination. It's a combination of all your experiences that build to the success you want. It's taking steps each day with God to bring forth that vision. It's pursuing aligned things and not busy work. It's knowing that this is not one and done. This is a lifestyle with You and God. Others will come in your life, but God has a special assignment for you.

REMOVE THE EXCUSES

You can make-up every excuse in the book. I could have told God that I haven't arrived, that I don't feel adequate, but I am. You are too! I do my best to speak life and to watch what I say. After thinking of all the money I invested which on the surface has not yielded the monetary return yet, I could think that God has stripped me of everything, but God hadn't. I was putting value on money versus every blessing and opportunity in the past and coming.

I have to immediately go back to gratitude. No, I'm not stripped of everything. Those decisions I made were with God and God led. I'm clear on that, so you must be clear on your decisions to help you in your next step.

The lost revenue and resources in the scope of God's future blessings for me and you are pennies to what God has in store for us. I'm blessed, you're blessed just look around. Watch what you say to yourself. Stripped away was not true. I placed money as the definition of being stripped from everything. Initially, I felt like I could have set my family up better (before I was let go from my day job), but I shifted my thoughts, through prayer, friends, advisors, and audio listening.

No one put this pressure on me. The projects I did were amazing and they impacted many, they were successful. My perspective had to shift.

I had to acknowledge truth versus letting the negativity sink in. We don't lack for anything. It's important to look over your life and see what you can do in this time to help you to create. Maybe it is working a day job or taking on an extra project. This is temporary. Consider this your investor.

The key here is to look for things aligned with what you seek to do. So as you are making an income to cover your idea, or pursuing higher education, can you also use that time to learn a skill? Consider this your investment.

Know that God is going to use everything you experience to strengthen you. You just have to know that and not belittle anything you do or have experienced.

Start with a new day. Continue to plant seeds and utilize the wisdom that God is providing you. You would not be reading this book if I wouldn't have started and persevered to release it. I've been releasing my God-given and sometimes man-made ideas since I was a teenager. It's why I can tell you to hold on to God in the face of adversity. I can also tell you that it all works out in the end. There is a power activated in you when you step out on faith.

Chapter 12

Take Steps Today

Creating with God is a life journey

Things will come in your path that you have to dodge, embrace, or kick out the way. There are times when you are leading and other times where you are not.

My father races in marathons. I've participated in a 5k race. I only did it to be with my father, but being in a race helped me understand the endurance it took to complete it, and that it's never really over. There is always another level, a next project, a new season and in life you take the breaks you need but you keep going, but with God not alone.

God is your secret weapon. He's a secret that you can share with others. Some will receive it and others will not. Make God part of your life every day.

Yes...a lifetime journey

This is a forever journey, not just one project that you do or a few ideas here and there, this is a life journey created with God. It isn't just creating your ideas to start a business, write a book, start a non-profit, or design a product.

Creating with God also looks at your personal time and where it goes, and it's creating memories with your family. It's being creative on solutions to things that come in your way, it's restructuring your life so that there is peace and an energetic flow. This doesn't mean that you will not experience challenging times, it just means that you know you're not alone and if God can show you how creative you are personally, there's no telling what you will have the confidence to pursue that can bring impact in your community and even throughout the world.

The biggest thing to remember is to do it with God. Keep God at the head of the conversations you are having and the decisions you are making.

Create with the Ultimate Creator

God is the ultimate creator. God is the creator of the universe and the creator of all things. He is the creator of you and I.

> Ephesians 2:10, (NIV) *"For we are God's handiwork, created in Christ Jesus to do good works, which God prepared in advance for us to do."*

We have to know this, so that as we create we do not step in front of God, try to manipulate or force things to come to fruition, but walk with God, in spirit and in truth, because God has already prepared us to do good works in him. That motivates me.

Tools

Nothing replaces prayer. Prayer is your direct communication to God. Here are tools you can use as reminders during your earthly battles.

You can operate from a place of heaven on earth.

> Matthew 6:9-10 (ESV) *"Our Father in heaven, hallowed be your name. Your kingdom come, your will be done, on earth as it is in heaven."*

Remember God is working on your behalf and He wants you to do what you can. In that, you have to protect your thoughts, beliefs, and take action.

11 Keys to Release the Creator in You

You can use these eleven keys on earth to release the creator in you. These keys don't take away from God's instructions, it is only a way to remind you of the areas to focus on.

1) Style and Curiosity

Embrace your style and how God designed you.

We each have our unique style and way we do things. We can each learn from each other, but do it our way.

By embracing your style you don't take things too seriously and it helps the creator in us to not look for permission from others but to be ourselves.

> Romans 12:2 (NIV) *"Do not be conformed to this age, but be transformed by the renewing of your mind, so that you may discern what is the good, pleasing, and perfect will of God."*

2) FAITH over fear

Believe and know you can do it and then do it, so when fear creeps up, you know God is with you, so you do not let fear take over.

Check in with yourself each day and acknowledge your emotions. Review how you're making decisions. Are these decisions in God or out of fear and anxiety? Place your cares and worries in God. That's where peace and clarity are. That's where when you see nothing, God shows you the abundance there.

> *"By faith we understand that the universe was formed at God's command, so that what is seen was not made out of what was visible."* Hebrews 11:3 (NIV)

3) Gratitude

Say out loud what you are grateful for. Say it to yourself what you are grateful for. Know it! Don't just say it to be saying it. Know what you are grateful for. This will help shift your perspective and make the journey more meaningful. This will help you to be what you are seeking, because you will know how blessed you are on this journey. It will also help you see solutions because you are open and not closing yourself up in doubt.

> *"Give thanks to the Lord for he is good, his love endures forever."* Psalm 118 (NIV)

4) Focus to Amplify

Have you ever been frustrated when you had nothing to do? Have you ever been frustrated when you were busy?

Either way, frustrations can occur and it's important to pursue aligned goals to move forward. This will help to amplify the creator in you.

> Philippians 4:6 (ESV), *"Do not be anxious about anything, but in everything by prayer and supplication with thanksgiving let your requests be made known to God."*

So what do you need to focus on? Maybe cleaning your space and once you clean your space you will now have a better environment to create.

The key is to focus on the right work, not busy work. Remind yourself of that. You will know when it's busy work when you look back over it and it didn't support your goals. You'll also know it as you are doing it. Will you ignore it or will you focus to amplify and set yourself up to release your creativity?

5) Rest, Enjoy and have FUN

God blessed us with beauty all around, explore it, and have fun. Bring heaven on earth. This helps to renew our thoughts and can also be a source of inspiration.

Make time to get away from mundane activities and use fresh air to relax. In nature, it seems to me like there is an abundance of time. Each plant or animal does what it is meant to do. We're the ones who overcomplicate things and care what others think. The plants and animals are created for a purpose and they are a good example of how to live with our innate desires and bring them to life.

> *"But ask the beasts, and they will teach you; the birds of the heavens, and they will tell you; or the bushes of the earth, and they will teach you; and the fish of the sea will declare to you. Who among all these does not know that the hand of the Lord has done this? In his hand is the life of every living thing and the breath of all mankind."* Job 12:7-10 (ESV)

Also, think about fun. Have you ever just watched a child play? They have no fear or worry. Be like a child and dream so big with God.

Our experiences shape our perspective and how we show-up.

This is why God's presence in our life is so important, so we do not limit our thinking.

The great thing is being creators and using creativity never goes away. Imagine if we continue to share these thoughts with our kids and as they grow they will be more attuned to God's power in their life, versus shying away from God because of not understanding how easy it is to come to God and to grow in God. Lastly, don't minimize the need to sleep and rest. This is so powerful for rejuvenation. God communicates with you in your sleep, so be mindful of what you watch and consume, so that Gods directions are clear to you.

6) Eliminate to Activate

Incorporate fasting in your walk with God to enable yourself to hear clearly what God is asking of you. Fasting is about getting closer to God.

This will help you pivot where needed, and know what to eliminate to create. Fasting will help you to focus on what is important and eliminate the noise. You can go online now and be bombarded with what you should be doing.

Start a business, go back to school, learn this funnel, no learn my process, focus on the money, no focus on the journey...... increase your love life while also cooking and cleaning and going after your dreams.... yadah yadah yadah. This can be overwhelming and cause confusion.

God will provide the answers and can also use your past as a guide to the wisdom you've developed.

> Proverbs 4:7, "Wisdom is the principal thing; therefore get wisdom: and with all thy getting get understanding."

By fasting, you can listen to God to get the understanding you are seeking or the understanding that God needs you to know in this time for God's next step for you.

7) Evaluate Your Surroundings and Expand Your Network

Everyone has a pursuit and gifts. By aligning with others in the spirit each one of you can bring your own greatness.

> Romans 12:6-8 (NIV) "Having gifts that differ according to the grace given to us, let us use them: if prophecy, in proportion to our faith; if service, in our serving; the one who teaches, in his teaching; the one who exhorts, in his exhortation; the one who contributes, in generosity; the one who leads, with zeal; the one who does acts of mercy, with cheerfulness."

Your gifts can work together.

Be open to getting involved with groups and organizations. Step outside your environment to look for inspiration and to meet other God led individuals.

Use discernment. Those that care will show it always through their actions. Also, they have their own goals and dreams and it's important for them to be in pursuit too and for you to show up for them, as you'd want in return.

Be there for others, but don't let that take over your time.

Also, be mindful when you are checking in with that person for the next steps and the answer versus asking God. God can use people to help guide you so, check-in on the answers you receive.

8) Quiet the Noise

Turn off the TV, unplug from social media. Listen to within.

Journal, brain dump by writing out your ideas, what you're feeling, experiencing, ideas, and thoughts.

This will help you release and focus.

Dedicate time to pray to God in a quiet area so you can hear more clearly and not be influenced (but know you can talk to God anytime). Practice talking to God. Eventually if not already, you will find yourself talking to God like you talk to your loved one anywhere and anytime. It will become normal.

God's message to you may not be loud it could come quietly. It may not come in a sign or miracle. It may not show up when you think it should. By daily getting in God's presence, it will help you discern your experiences.

"He says, 'Be still, and know that I am God." Psalm 46:10 (NIV)

9) Turn Obstacles into Opportunities

Think about a time when you experienced an obstacle. What examples of God's grace did you experience? Remember those.

This time also creates a window of opportunity for the creation of newness. We may think that our past defines us, but we are new creations in God.

If it seems like everything is falling apart, it's actually a set-up to something great but God needs to position you in another way that will serve you better.

> Jeremiah 1:19 (NIV) *"They will fight against you, but they will not overcome you, for I am with you to deliver you," declares the Lord."*

Creativity is in our very being. By keeping our heart and mind on God we become stronger in it and grow our ability to bring forth our ideas.

The great ascended Maya Angelou stated that thinking creatively helps foster even greater creativity, *"You can't use up creativity,"* she says *"The more you use, the more you have."*

10) Abundance is Your Birthright

Eradicate the idea that you do not have the money to create your God-goal. The focus on lack and creating cannot exist together. If you battle both in your mind, you will create decisions from that place, versus a place of faith.

I'm not sure what you were taught about money, but know that money is not the root of all evil. Yes, people can make bad and evil decisions regarding money. So God needs us to utilize money as a tool to create change, impact, and legacy.

Just like any other area of your life, don't put money first. Keep God first and the resources you need will come. Also, depending on how you feel about money, there can be tension around money. I've felt tension around money before, so prayer is key. When you're creating these grand God visions, your energy has to exude confidence in it. Set your price and follow God's direction.

It's one thing to be transparent and to acknowledge what you physically see, but God already knows what you have and because you desire this goal wholeheartedly to bring forth God's vision, it is a priority to God to get you the resources you need for it. So dream big and let God evolve it. Have faith that the vision is unfolding and that it will be bigger than what you could have imagined.

> Ephesians 3:20 (NIV) *"Now to him who is able to do immeasurably more than all we ask or imagine, according to his power that is at work within us."*

My Prayer for You

I pray that as you walk through each day, you show up as the divine creation God made you to be. That you walk with God and not try to make it happen or do it on your own. Know your goals and dreams are insights to the vision God has over your life and you are enough! You have what you need right now to get started. Trust God's timing and know God is above ALL people and ANY decision. God has some great things in store for you and those who are connected to you because you believe and flow in faith. I pray you continue to put out love into the world and remember as your life evolves that God is always with you and will work things out for your good. AMEN!

11) Don't Create it! Create with God.

This whole time you have been telling me to create it. No, I have been encouraging you to create with God. Creating only the things you are meant to. Don't walk around scared trying to figure it out or think you need to create every idea popping in your head. Establish your main goals, pursue aligned tasks and make today your best day. You will know what your next step is. BE IT, DO IT, but with God.

What's Next?

You live in the NOW. There is no set check-list. Pray, take care of yourself and do <u>your</u> next steps. AGAIN, don't force anything. Let God work, be what you are expecting, give lots of love, take the next step, get some rest and repeat all.

To connect with other creators on God's mission, like "Year of the Creator" on Facebook and Instagram @yearofthecreator or visit yearofthecreator.com

Thank you!

Year of the Creator is dedicated to my husband Antonio. You have supported me since we were teenagers. I know that I create even more with a fierceness because of your support and reminders of what's important.

To my son, whom I pray he always knows that God is with him and made him extraordinary so dream big and don't limit God (along with any future kids).

To my parents who gave me a great foundation full of love and the space to go after my dreams.

To my grandma who reminds me, "to just do it, man!"

To Poppe of Indy Design Week—thank you for creating an opportunity for me to be a guest speaker. I felt strongly in my spirit to write this book and when you chose this topic out of several ideas I submitted. It made me accelerate completing the outline and presentation. The book has now evolved from the talk, so thank you.

To Day Edwards for creating Prayers for the Boss Babes. That project helped me dive deeper into creating with God. Along with provided encouragement and insight on releasing a book.

To Angel Santos for your tough, yet caring approach to writing the Year of the Creator. Hiring you, redirected my focus, provided a strategy and made it easier for me to get Year of the Creator to the market.

To Michael and Elliot for helping me expand my thinking to further my mission. You both have showed me how to dive deeper into God's word and to show-up in that grace and power.

To YOU and my FAMILY for reading and supporting me to help more creatives release their ideas. THANK YOU!

About the Year of the Creator

The ULTIMATE way to create your ideas, "YEAR OF THE CREATOR" presents no fluff and simple ways to create with God each day.

Life evolves and it's important to know that you were created extraordinary and have the power to create, in your everyday life and in your ideas. They go hand in hand. You must know you are a creator! Give yourself permission to experience Gods presence and create with God. I'm excited about what you are and will create.

GOD is......
the ultimate creator.
the ultimate healer.
the ultimate bank.
the ultimate networker.
the ultimate provider.
the ultimate decision maker.
the ultimate anything you need.

How to connect:

Visit www.yearofthecreator.com

Join the Facebook community of creators at facebook.com/yearofthecreator

Tag @yearofthecreator on social media

email info@yearofthecreator.com

We'd love to follow your journey.

About the Author

At 15 years old, Denisha Ferguson produced her first fashion and hair show with $250 she had saved. Since then, God has led her to produce fashion shows as a platform in Indiana for creators in Indiana and across the world. Now, she has over 20 plus years of experience in event production, research, project managing, and fashion design and serves as the CEO of the Indiana Fashion Foundation and Indiana Fashion Week and also the Creative Director and Designer of Dlang Designs.

She believes FASHION is a vessel for her to inspire and motivate others to pursue their God-given creativity.

She has an Associate's in Fashion Merchandising, Bachelors in Business Management, and an MBA. While she values her education, she is quick to tell others she has learned more by doing and being it.

In fact, one of her favorite original quotes is "Creativity is in our DNA and each one of us is born with it, which makes us creators. Let's serve in that place to make impact, income and build legacy!"

You can find out more about Denisha at denishaferguson.com & yearofthecreator.com.

www.ingramcontent.com/pod-product-compliance
Lightning Source LLC
Chambersburg PA
CBHW061944220426
43662CB00012B/2024